Zany Facts for Smart Kids from the World of Animals, Birds and Insects
© 2023 by Dr. Leo Lexicon

Notice of Rights

All rights reserved. No portion of this publication may be reproduced, distributed, or transmitted in any form or by any means, electronic or mechanical, including photocopying, recording, or any information storage and retrieval system, without prior written permission from the author. Reproduction or translation of this work in any form beyond that permitted by Sections 107 or 108 of the 1976 United States Copyright Act is strictly prohibited. No companion books, summaries, or study guides are authorized under this notice. For other permission requests, please contact the author.

Liability Disclaimer

The information provided within this book is for general informational purposes only. While every effort has been made to keep the information up-to-date and correct, there are no representations or warranties, express or implied, about the completeness, accuracy, reliability, suitability, or availability with respect to the information, products, services, or related graphics contained in this book for any purpose. Any use of this information is at your own risk.

This book is not intended to be, nor should the user consider it to be, medical, legal, or business advice for any situation. The information provided in this book is not intended to diagnose, treat, cure, or prevent any disease or medical condition. The author and publisher disclaim any liability, loss, or risk, personal or otherwise, that is incurred as a consequence, directly or indirectly, of the use and application of any of the contents of this book. Readers are solely responsible for their actions and decisions based on the information presented in this book. It is important to note that the information provided in this book is not intended to replace professional medical advice or treatment. Readers are advised that any decisions related to their health and well-being should be made in consultation with qualified healthcare professionals.

This book may contain affiliate links. It is important to note that the author only recommends products or services that they genuinely believe will be beneficial to the reader. In order to ensure trust and transparency, this disclosure complies with the rules set by the Federal Trade Commission. The support received through these affiliate links helps sustain the creation of valuable content. We appreciate the understanding and support of all readers.

The author, company, and publisher shall in no event be held liable for any loss or other damages, including but not limited to special, incidental, consequential, or other damages. This disclaimer applies to any damages caused by any failure of performance, error, omission, interruption, deletion, delay in transmission or transmission, defect, computer malware, communication line failure, theft, destruction, or unauthorized access to or use of records, whether for breach of contract, tort, negligence, or under any other cause of action. By reading this book, you agree to use the contents entirely at your own risk and that you are solely responsible for your use of the contents. The author, company, and publisher do not warrant the performance or applicability of any references listed in this book. All references and links are for informational purposes only and are not warranted for content, accuracy, or any other implied or explicit purpose.

Check out our fun, auto-themed coloring books

Hours of coloring fun for all ages!

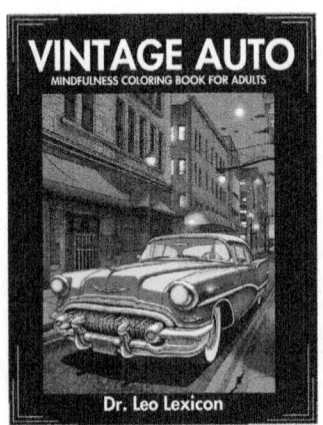

- Each book has over 40+ carefully curated HQ images
- Pefect companion for a road trip or vacation
- Try one today, you won't be disappointed
- Check out our other titles, we have all ages covered
- From the team at Lexicon Labs, bringing joy one page at a time!
- Follow Dr. Leo Lexicon on Twitter

 @LeoLexicon

LEXICON LABS

Zany Facts for Smart Kids
From the World of Animals, Birds and Insects

by

Dr. Leo Lexicon

CONTENTS

Chapter 1: Amazing Mammals..2

Chapter 2: Fantastic Birds 12

Chapter 3: Creepy Crawly Critters 19

Chapter 4: Slithering Snakes 27

Chapter 5: Jumping Frogs 34

Chapter 6: Swimming Fish..42

Chapter 7: Extinct Beasts 48

EXTRA! Excerpt from AI for Smart Kids Ages 6-9 ...60

Zany Facts for Smart Kids

From the World of Animals, Birds and Insects

Looking to amaze your friends and stump your teachers? Get ready to become the most clever know-it-all with this jam-packed book of the craziest animal facts!

From shaggy wooly mammoths with tusks so huge they had to shovel snow with them to velociraptors that eviscerated prey with their vicious ankle claws, this book covers all the deadly dinosaurs and extinct beasts you need to terrify your classmates.

Learn how the Megalodon shark could bite a school bus in half with choppers the size of bowling balls. Or how the giant ground sloth was like a 20-foot long living tank covered in armor. Heck, you will even discover hell pigs the size of a rhino!

This book is also packed with unbelievable facts about the most mind-boggling bugs, fish, snakes, and frogs alive today. Did you know the Goliath frog is over a foot long and weighs more than some newborn babies? Or that the golden poison dart frog has enough toxins to kill 100,000 people? You'll even learn about electric eels that zap with 860 volts and archerfish that shoot water to knock down bugs.

So get ready to amaze your friends and bewilder your teachers with the strangest animal facts on planet Earth! This book will make you the most unexpected genius in school—guaranteed! In each of the seven chapters that follow, you will find bulleted lists of zany facts that will make your head spin. And remember, though many of these facts are utterly unbelievable, they are true!

Dr. Leo Lexicon is an educator and author. He is the founder of Lexicon Labs, a publishing imprint that is focused on creating entertaining books for active minds.

ZANY FACTS FOR SMART KIDS

Chapter 1: Amazing Mammals

- The fingerprints of a koala bear are so indistinguishable from those of humans that they have, on occasion, been confused at a crime scene.
- An elephant's trunk contains over 40,000 muscles.
- A blue whale's tongue weighs as much as an entire adult elephant. The tongue can weigh up to 5,000 pounds (2,268 kg)!
- Dogs have a sense of time. It's been proven that they know the difference between an hour and five.
- Cats can jump up to seven times their length.
- Bats are the only mammals that can actually fly.

- The earliest ancestors of whales and dolphins were four-footed land animals.
- Elephants use their tusks to dig for food and water.
- Skunks can accurately spray their smelly fluid up to 10 feet.
- The scientific name for the red fox is Vulpes vulpes, meaning "true fox" in Latin.
- Polar bears have black skin under their transparent fur, which helps absorb heat from the sun.
- Hippos secrete a red substance that was once thought to be sweat but is actually a natural sunblock.
- The Giant Anteater is mostly silent but can make a humming sound and 35 different vocalizations.
- Platypuses don't have stomachs; their esophagus connects directly to their intestines.
- Bats use echolocation, emitting sounds too high for humans to hear and listening for echoes to navigate.
- Elephants communicate using infrasonic vocalizations below human hearing range.
- Giraffes have blue tongues, which may serve an antimicrobial function.
- The scientific name for the walrus, Odobenus rosmarus, is Latin for "tooth-walking sea horse".
- Raccoons are extremely dexterous, using their paws to latch doors, open jars, and untie knots.
- The moose is the largest deer species, and the male's antlers can weigh over 40 pounds when fully grown.
- The scientific name for the killer whale, Orcinus orca, refers to the underworld in Roman mythology.
- Manatees are informally called sea cows, but they are actually marine mammals more closely related to elephants.

- Lemurs groom each other to reinforce social bonds, with females often taking the initiative.
- Otters hold hands while sleeping so they don't drift apart on the water's surface.
- Kangaroos keep growing throughout their lives, so the biggest kangaroos are the oldest.
- Giraffes only need 5–30 minutes of sleep in a 24-hour period.
- Sloths can hold their breath longer than dolphins.
- The sleeping habits of dolphins are still largely unknown, since they rarely show any external signs of sleep.
- Elephants' brains react to humans the same way that human brains react to puppies – they think we're cute!
- Hippos milk is bright pink.
- An elephant can use its tusks to dig for groundwater. An adult elephant needs to drink around 210 liters of water a day.
- Camels have three eyelids to protect themselves from blowing sand.
- Almost half of the over 200 breeds of dogs recognized worldwide originated in Europe.
- Manatees are also known as sea cows.
- A polar bear's fur is not white. It's actually transparent, and their black skin absorbs heat from the sun.
- The giant panda typically eats over 25 different species of bamboo.
- Otters have the world's thickest fur, with over 1 million hairs per square inch.
- Lions sleep 16–20 hours a day.
- Cheetahs are the fastest land animals and can reach speeds up to 70 mph.

- Baby elephants suck their trunks for comfort, much like humans suck their thumbs.
- A rhinoceros horn is not a true horn, but is made of keratin, the same material that makes up hair and fingernails.
- Orangutans build a new nest every night from branches and foliage.
- The echidna is a spiny anteater that lays eggs like a reptile but is actually a mammal.
- Walruses have the longest tusks of any animal, with tusks reaching up to 3 feet long.
- Lemurs groom each other as a sign of affection, similar to how monkeys socialize.
- Horses and rabbits can't vomit.
- Chipmunks have pouches in their cheeks to carry food back to their burrows.
- The scientific name for the western lowland gorilla is Gorilla gorilla gorilla.
- Orcas, also known as killer whales, are actually a type of dolphin.
- An adult lion's roar can be heard up to 5 miles away.
- Dolphins give each other distinct names.
- Elephants have been known to rescue other animals, like trapped dogs and baby rhinos.
- Male seahorses get pregnant and give birth to baby seahorses.
- The capybara is the largest living rodent in the world.
- The gestation period of an African elephant is 22 months, the longest of any land animal.
- The spot pattern on every giraffe is completely unique, like a human fingerprint.
- Koalas sleep around 18–22 hours per day.

- Grizzly bears can run as fast as 35 mph. Never try to outrun one!
- Beluga whales in captivity have been known to play fetch with objects thrown by humans.
- The scientific name for the giant armadillo is Priodontes maximus, which means "giant toothed one."
- Manatees swim at a maximum speed of around 15 mph.
- Moles have a special extra thumb called a prepollex that helps them dig.
- The mouth of a camel has three sets of eyelids and two rows of long eyelashes to keep sand out of their eyes.
- When threatened, porcupines stamp their feet and click their quills to warn predators away.
- Bat pups can consume 100% of their body weight daily in milk.
- Elephants use infrasonic vocalizations that are too low for humans to hear to communicate with each other.
- The Maned Wolf is the largest canid in South America and has long legs to see over tall grass.
- Echidnas are covered with fur and spines. They are the only mammals that lay eggs.
- Jaguars have the strongest bite force of any big cat and can bite through turtle shells.
- Bears have an incredible sense of smell that is seven times better than a bloodhound's.
- Red pandas use their bushy tails for balance, wrapping them around tree branches as they climb.
- Dolphins develop complex relationships and can coordinate their swimming and breathing.
- The scientific name for the giant panda is Ailuropoda melanoleuca, which means "black and white cat-foot."

- Sea otters hold hands while sleeping so they don't drift apart.
- The average dairy cow produces around 6.3 gallons of milk per day.
- A skunk's spray can reach distances up to 10 feet with precision.
- Wolverines have very strong jaws and can crush bones and eat frozen meat.
- Dogs have specialized muscles around their eyes that allow them to make expressive faces.
- The Incas domesticated llamas and used them as pack animals to transport goods.
- Horses kick both front and back, but their back legs are stronger and cause more injury.
- Tiger urine smells like buttered popcorn because of the fatty acids in it.
- Female ferrets will die if they do not mate. Prolonged estrogen production without pregnancy causes fatal anemia.
- The scientific name for the Southern Tamandua anteater is Tamandua tetradactyla, which means "four-fingered."
- The tail of a beaver is paddle-shaped for propelling itself through water and steering.
- Lemurs have a structure called a toilet claw that aids in their grooming routines.
- A cat's pancreas does not produce enough insulin, so they cannot properly digest sugar and sweets.
- Sea turtles have special glands that remove salt from the water they drink and concentrate salt from the food they eat.
- Golden hamsters are not originally golden. Selective breeding made them that color for the pet industry.

- The fossa is a cat-like animal native to Madagascar and a member of the mongoose family.
- Grizzly bears enter a hibernation-like state in winter, but do not truly hibernate and can wake easily.
- Moose antlers can grow up to an inch per day and weigh over 40 pounds when fully grown.
- Camels can close their nostrils during sandstorms.
- An elephant can smell water up to 3 miles away.
- A cow gives nearly 200,000 glasses of milk in her lifetime.
- Dolphins can hold their breath for over 10 minutes and dive to depths of over 300 meters.
- The African crested porcupine has the longest quills, measuring over 20 inches.
- Manatees are sometimes called sea cows, but they are actually closely related to elephants.
- The hoatzin is the only bird with foregut fermentation like cows, allowing it to digest leaves.
- The name "puma" comes from the Peruvian Quechua language, meaning "powerful animal."
- Orcas have different diets. Resident orcas mainly eat fish, while transient orcas hunt marine mammals.
- When defending against predators, a skunk will first stamp its feet as a warning.
- The tapetum lucidum behind a cat's retina reflects light back through the eye, improving night vision.
- The scientific name of the giant armadillo is Priodontes maximus, meaning "giant toothed one."
- Lemurs groom each other to reinforce social bonds, with females often taking the initiative.
- The pygmy marmoset is the smallest monkey and can stand on an adult's thumbnail.

- River otters have webbed feet, water-repellent fur, and can hold their breath for up to 8 minutes.
- The gestation period of an Asian elephant is 18-22 months, the longest of any land mammal.
- A hippo's closest living relatives are cetaceans - whales, dolphins and porpoises.
- Raccoons have sensitive front paws that are protected by a thin furred mask when searching for food.
- The claws of big cats like lions and tigers retract when at rest so they stay sharp.
- The bovine family includes cows, buffaloes, bison, yaks, and antelopes.
- Aardvarks have narrow snouts, long sticky tongues, strong claws and special teeth to eat ants and termites.
- Lemurs are arboreal, spending most of their time in trees. They have flexible ankles that allow them to run along branches.
- Capybaras are highly social and live in groups of 10–20 individuals with one dominant male.
- Pangolins have protective keratin scales covering their skin and can roll into a ball when threatened.
- Tigers are solitary hunters and will travel many miles to find prey, eating up to 60 pounds at one time.
- Opossums are marsupials, carrying newborns in a pouch until they are old enough to live independently.
- The aardvark's name comes from the Afrikaans word for "earth pig." They have pig-like snouts and strong claws for digging.
- Elephants use infrasonic vocalizations below human hearing range to communicate over long distances.
- Dolphins have signature whistles for individual identification and can mimic human speech.

- Lemurs groom each other frequently to reinforce social bonds, with females often taking the initiative.
- The scientific name for the giant panda, Ailuropoda melanoleuca, means "black and white cat-foot" in Greek.
- Opossums have opposable thumbs on their rear feet and a prehensile tail to grip branches.
- Moose antlers grow rapidly up to an inch per day and can weigh over 40 pounds when fully grown.

Chapter 2: Fantastic Birds

- Hummingbirds are the only birds that can fly backward.
- The ostrich is the largest bird in the world and can grow over 9 feet tall.
- Penguin feet have special blood vessels that prevent them from freezing in the extreme cold.
- The longest recorded non-stop bird flight was 7 days by a swift bird.
- Woodpeckers have specially reinforced skulls to absorb the impact of pecking wood.

- Flamingos get their pink color from pigments in the algae and crustaceans they eat.
- Owls can turn their heads 270 degrees, but cannot move their eyes inside their heads.
- The extinct elephant bird was over 10 feet tall and laid eggs with a capacity of 2.5 gallons, the largest of any bird ever known.
- Vultures have very acidic stomach acids that allow them to safely digest rotting carcasses.
- Toucans have bills almost as long as their bodies, but they are very light due to their honeycombed internal structure.
- The bee hummingbird is the smallest bird, only 2 inches long and weighing less than a penny.
- Birds like albatrosses can sleep while flying by resting one brain hemisphere at a time.
- Ravens can mimic human speech and make sounds like car horns.
- Secretary birds specialize in stomping snakes to death with their strong legs before eating them.
- The legendary thunderbird was said to create thunder by flapping its wings and lightning when blinking its eyes.
- The ostrich is the largest bird and can grow over 9 feet tall and weigh over 300 pounds.
- The Kiwi is the only bird with nostrils at the end of its beak instead of the base.
- Flamingos get their pink color from pigments in the algae and crustaceans they eat.
- Woodpeckers have barbed tongues that can extend up to 5 inches to spear insects.
- Pelicans have stretchy pouches that can hold up to 3 gallons of fish and water.

- Penguins huddle together in large groups to stay warm in extreme cold temperatures.
- Some migrating birds fly incredible distances - arctic terns travel over 40,000 miles annually.
- The extinct moa was an enormous flightless bird that grew over 12 feet tall and weighed 500 pounds.
- Vultures have very acidic stomach juices that allow them to safely digest rotting and diseased carcasses.
- Hornbills are recognizable by their long, downward-curving bills and eyelashes.
- The ostrich is the fastest running bird and can sprint up to 45 miles per hour.
- Some birds, like the albatross, can sleep while flying by resting each hemisphere of their brain in turn.
- Woodcocks have specially designed bill tips that allow them to grasp earthworms underground.
- The cassowary is an enormous flightless bird that can grow over 6 feet tall and weigh 130 pounds.
- Secretary birds specialize in killing snakes by trampling and kicking them before eating them.
- The extinct elephant bird was over 10 feet tall and laid eggs with a capacity of 2.5 gallons.
- Birds like the horned screamer have plate-like structures on their wings that produce a distinctive whirring sound when flying.
- Penguins have more feathers per square inch than any other bird, which helps insulate them in frigid climates.
- The legendary thunderbird in Native American folklore was said to create thunder by flapping its wings.
- Turkey vultures release vomit as a defense mechanism against predators. The vomit irritates skin and can sting if it gets in your eyes.

- The bee hummingbird beats its wings up to 80 times per second, making a humming noise.
- Woodcocks have specially designed bill tips that can open and close, allowing them to grasp earthworms underground.
- Hornbills are recognizable by their long, downward-curving bills, which have slight helical construction to add strength.
- Flamingos build mud mounds for their nests. The height protects their eggs when seasonal floods come.
- Birds like the ostrich and emu have long eyelashes that help keep sand and dust out of their eyes.
- The legendary phoenix is a mythological fire bird that cyclically regenerated by arising from the ashes of its predecessor.
- Ravens are among the smartest birds, with problem-solving abilities similar to those of great apes and human children.
- The extinct moa was an enormous flightless bird that grew over 12 feet tall and weighed up to 500 pounds.
- Hornbills build nests inside hollowed-out tree trunks that are sealed shut, except for a narrow slit through which the female receives food.
- The kakapo is the world's only flightless parrot and has legs adapted for climbing trees instead of wings for flying.
- Flamingos build mud mounds for their nests to protect their eggs when seasonal floods come through their habitat.
- The bee hummingbird beats its tiny wings up to 80 times per second, creating the distinctive humming noise.
- Pelicans have stretchy throat pouches that can hold up to 3 gallons of fish and water when feeding.

- Penguins form large, densely packed huddles, with each bird facing inward to share warmth in extreme cold temperatures.
- Hummingbirds have the fastest metabolism of all animals - their hearts beat up to 1,260 times per minute.
- Blue jays rub ants on their feathers to act as a natural insect repellent. The ants secrete an acidic substance when agitated.
- Blue jays are known for their intelligence and complex social behaviors. They can mimic hawk calls as alarms and other bird sounds.
- Sparrows can live for up to 10 years, quite a long time for a small songbird.
- There are 29 recognized species of sparrow in North America alone. They come in different sizes and plumage colors.
- Male birds-of-paradise perform elaborate song and dance displays, showing off bright plumage to attract mates.
- The Eurasian tree sparrow has been observed using cigarette butts in its nest to repel mites and parasites.
- Goldfinches line their nests with thistle down, plant fibers, and animal hair to cushion eggs and hatchlings.
- Chickadees can lower their body temperatures by 10–12 °F on cold winter nights to conserve energy.
- Nuthatches are the only bird species known to smear mud on their nest entrance as an insect repellent.
- Carolina wrens sing duets to defend territories and strengthen pair bonds. Males perform most calls, and females respond.
- Crows are known to hold grudges against specific human faces associated with threatening behavior toward them.

Chapter 3: Creepy Crawly Critters

- The Goliath birdeater tarantula has a leg span up to 12 inches wide, making it the largest spider in the world.
- Jumping spiders have excellent eyesight and can leap up to 50 times their own body length.
- Butterflies taste with their feet and have taste receptors on their legs.
- Bullet ants get their name because their sting is as painful as getting shot with a bullet.
- Ants can lift objects 50 times heavier than their own body weight.

- The Hercules beetle is one of the world's strongest creatures relative to body size, able to carry 850 times its own weight.
- Houseflies hum in the key of F.
- A queen termite can lay up to 30,000 eggs per day.
- Praying mantises are the only insects that can turn their heads and look over their shoulders.
- Millipedes have two pairs of legs per body segment, unlike centipedes, which have just one.
- Caterpillars have up to 4,000 muscles in their bodies, compared to humans, which have just 639.
- The heaviest insect in the world is the Little Barrier Island giant weta, which weighs about 2.5 ounces.
- Silk produced by spiders is stronger than steel thread of the same thickness.
- The average house spider eats around 2,000 insects a year, helping keep other pest populations under control.
- Male fireflies use their flashing light patterns to signal and attract females.
- The bombardier beetle can spray a hot, noxious chemical spray from its abdomen when threatened, with a popping sound.
- Fleas can jump up to 200 times their own height, the equivalent of a 6-foot-tall human jumping over the Empire State Building.
- A honeybee visits 50–100 flowers during one collection trip from the hive.
- Butterflies taste food by standing on top of it; they cannot eat unless they can stand on their food source.
- The vicious warrior wasp gets its name from its habit of fighting with other insects and stealing their prey.
- Some caterpillars inflate their heads to mimic snakes when threatened.

- The goliath birdeater tarantula has fangs so large they can puncture human skin.
- Dragonflies have compound eyes with up to 30,000 lenses, allowing them to see in nearly all directions.
- Stick insects and leaf insects are masters of camouflage, blending in with their surroundings.
- Spider silk is one of the strongest natural fibers and is being studied to make bulletproof vests.
- Dung beetles can pull 1,141 times their own body weight—the equivalent of a 70 kg human pulling 80 tons.
- The honeypot ant uses its own body to store liquid food for the rest of the colony, acting as a living larder.
- The Madagascar hissing cockroach produces a hissing sound by forcing air through its breathing holes.
- The snakefly resembles a dragonfly with a long nose and appears to slither like a snake when in flight.
- The diving bell spider builds an underwater air chamber with silk webs to breathe oxygen while remaining submerged for up to 24 hours.
- The giant burrowing cockroach reaches 6 inches long and can hiss loudly when threatened.
- The assassin bug carries corpses of its prey on its back as camouflage from predators.
- The Atlas moth is one of the world's largest insects, with a wingspan up to 1 foot wide.
- The wheel spider cartwheels down sand dunes in the Sahara desert to escape predators.
- The Venus flytrap secretes nectar on its open "jaws" to lure insects before trapping and digesting them.
- The orchid mantis perfectly mimics colorful orchid flowers, attracting unsuspecting insects to their deaths.
- The stinkhorn fungus gets its name from the foul, rotten meat smell it releases to attract flies.

- The tarantula hawk wasp has an extremely painful sting that it uses to paralyze tarantulas before dragging them to its nest as food for its larvae.
- The praying mantis is the only insect that can rotate its head 180 degrees to scan for predators and prey.
- Orb weaver spiders recycle their webs by eating them every night and spinning new ones the next day.
- The house centipede has 15 pairs of legs, while millipedes can have over 100 legs.
- Bombardier beetles can shoot boiling-hot chemical spray from their abdomens when threatened.
- Adults of the goliath beetle species can grow up to 4.5 inches long and weigh up to 3.5 ounces.
- The Darwin bark spider spins the largest known orb webs, with anchor lines spanning 25 meters across rivers.
- The diving bell spider fills its underwater bubble with air carried from the surface by trapping air in the hairs on its abdomen and legs.
- The assassin bug carries a corpse "backpack" as camouflage to sneak up on its prey without detection.
- The giant wetapunga in New Zealand hisses ominously when disturbed and exudes a vile odor.
- The emerald cockroach wasp stings and paralyzes cockroaches, then lays its eggs inside the body so its larvae can feed on the still-living roach.
- The Hummingbird hawkmoth hovers and drinks nectar from flowers just like a hummingbird, using its long proboscis.
- Vegetable caterpillars can shoot acid from knee-like joints up to 5 inches when threatened.
- The goliath bird-eating spider has microscopic hairs on its feet that can detect vibrations from insects walking nearby.

- Driver ants swarm through the jungle in groups of up to 50 million, devouring everything in their path.
- The assassin bug wears a "backpack" made from the corpses of its prey to help conceal itself from potential victims.
- The Atlas beetle is named after the Titan Atlas from Greek mythology because it can lift over 850 times its own body weight.
- The predaceous diving beetle hunts underwater using a bubble of air trapped against its wings as an oxygen supply.
- Click beetles can leap into the air with a loud "click" and flip themselves over if they get stuck on their backs.
- The wheel spider propels itself down sand dunes by cartwheeling down slopes to escape predators.
- The Australian spiny leaf insect perfectly resembles a eucalyptus leaf, down to the markings and spines.
- Daddy longlegs spiders have toxic venom but cannot bite humans due to their short fangs and small mouthparts.
- The marbled crayfish is a mutant species that clones itself through parthenogenesis, so all members of the species are female.
- The velvet worm subdues its prey by shooting an adhesive slime that immobilizes victims and entombs them.
- The giant wetapunga hisses loudly when disturbed and exudes a vile, stinking fluid from its joints as a defense.
- The golden tortoise beetle changes color from gold to red when alarmed, confusing its predators.
- The orchid mantis sways like the petals of the orchid flower it resembles to attract insect prey.
- The dragonhunter wasp catches and eats dragonflies and other insects mid-flight using its long legs.

- The stink bug releases a foul stench from its scent glands when threatened to deter predators.
- The beetle's elytra, or hard outer wings, are lined with many small hairs that are sensitive to even the slightest airflow, helping the beetle stabilize its flight.
- The parasitic horsehair worm develops inside grasshoppers and mind-controls its host into jumping into water so the mature worm can leave and reproduce.
- The emerald cockroach wasp delivers a targeted sting to a cockroach's brain that turns the roach into a zombie slave, which follows it back to its nest.
- The bombardier beetle can spray a boiling hot, high-pressure jet of irritant spray from its abdomen when threatened.
- The orchid mantis is camouflaged to look exactly like a pink orchid flower, attracting unsuspecting insects to their doom.
- The froghopper can leap 100 times its body length, the equivalent of a human jumping over 30 city blocks.
- The dance fly waves its wings up and down to imitate the motion of bees and wasps, allowing it to get close to prey.
- The venom of the Sydney funnel-web spider can kill a human in 15 minutes, but no deaths have occurred since antivenom was created.
- The spider wasp stings and paralyzes spiders before laying an egg on their bodies so the larva can feed on the still living spider.
- The velvet worm captures prey by ejecting slime out of nozzles on its body, entombing victims in quick-hardening glue.
- The tree lobster insect was thought extinct but was rediscovered in the 1960s, perched high up in the canopy of a single remaining tree.

- The diving bell spider builds an underwater air chamber with silk webs, allowing it to stay submerged for up to 24 hours while hunting.
- The tailor ant weaves leaves together using silk to create cozy nests for colonies of up to millions of ants.
- The assassin bug carries a "backpack" of camouflage made from the corpses of its prey to help avoid detection.
- The Hummingbird Hawk-moth hovers and drinks nectar from flowers just like a hummingbird, using its long proboscis tongue.
- The garden tiger moth caterpillar has spikes and hairs that sting and irritate predators if touched or eaten.
- The velvet ant is actually a wingless female wasp that is covered in red hairs and administers a painful sting.
- The diving bell spider builds a silk bubble under water that it fills with air from the surface, allowing it to remain submerged for over a day.
- The elephant mosquito has a proboscis long enough to pierce through clothing and sucks blood from humans and animals.
- The transient firefly synchronizes its blinking light patterns with others of its species to create impressive bioluminescent displays.
- The Australian peacock spider waves its colorful flaps and patters its legs during mating dances to attract females.
- The vicious warrior wasp earned its name by invading other insects' colonies to fight adults and carry off their larvae.
- The Satanic leaf-tailed gecko has flattened body and leaf-like lobes to camouflage itself as a dead leaf hanging in the jungle.

- The parasitic horsehair worm develops inside crickets and then mind-controls its host into jumping into water so it can emerge.
- The tree lobster was rediscovered in the 1960s after being thought extinct for 80 years, clinging high up in the canopy of one tree.
- The giant Lord Howe Island stick insect was also rediscovered after being considered extinct for over 80 years.

Chapter 4: Slithering Snakes

- The king cobra is the world's longest venomous snake, growing up to 18 feet long.
- Anacondas are semi-aquatic snakes found in tropical South America that can grow over 30 feet long.
- Rattlesnakes get their name from the rattle at the end of their tail, which they shake to warn off predators.
- The inland taipan of Australia is considered the most venomous snake in the world based on the toxicity of its venom.
- Pythons are nonvenomous constrictor snakes that subdue prey by coiling their bodies around victims and squeezing tightly.
- The black mamba of Africa is the fastest land snake in the world, capable of moving 12 mph at full speed.

- Sea snakes have paddle-like tails that help them swim efficiently through tropical ocean waters, hunting for fish.
- Cobras are venomous snakes capable of extending the ribs behind their heads into a signature hood when threatened.
- Viper snakes have long, hollow fangs that inject their victims with venom when they strike and bite.
- The boomslang snake of Africa gets its name from the Afrikaans words meaning "tree snake".
- The twig snake's thin body and beige color allow it to disguise itself perfectly as a dead stick in its tropical forest habitats.
- The snake detection theory suggests that humans and primates evolved with an innate fear of snakes over millennia.
- Pit vipers, like rattlesnakes, have heat-sensing pits on their faces to detect the body heat of warm-blooded prey.
- The bushmaster snake has the longest venomous fangs, measuring up to 2 inches long.
- Snakes smell using their forked tongues, which pick up scent particles and pass them to a special organ in the mouth.
- Snake venom comes in two main types: neurotoxic, which attacks the nervous system, and hemotoxic, which destroys red blood cells.
- The emerald tree boa of the Amazon has specially shaped teeth for gripping birds and other tree-dwelling prey.
- Snake muscles do not need to be anchored to bone, so they can flexibly open their jaws incredibly wide to swallow large prey.
- Snakes have slower metabolisms than mammals, allowing them to survive on just 12 to 15 meals per year.
- Spitting cobras can project their venom up to 8 feet away, aimed at the eyes or faces of threats.

- The common garter snake is one of the snakes most adapted to cold climates, found as far north as Alaska and Canada.
- The king cobra is the world's longest venomous snake, capable of reaching 18 feet in length.
- Rattlesnakes shake their tail rapidly to make a buzzing rattle sound as a warning to predators or intruders.
- Pythons and boas kill their prey by constriction, coiling their bodies tightly around the victim's chest to suffocate it.
- Pit vipers like rattlesnakes and copperheads have heat-sensing pits on their heads to detect and target warm-blooded prey.
- Cobras can flare out the skin behind their heads into a signature hood shape when threatened.
- The black mamba is the fastest land snake in the world, capable of reaching speeds over 12 miles per hour.
- Sea snakes have paddle-shaped tails that help them swim efficiently through tropical ocean waters while hunting fish.
- The twig snake's extremely thin body and beige coloration allow it to disguise itself as a dead stick in the jungle.
- Venomous coral snakes have a powerful neurotoxic venom that paralyzes nerve cells and shuts down breathing.
- The bushmaster snake has the longest venom fangs, measuring up to 2 inches long.
- The king cobra is capable of raising one-third of its body off the ground and looking a full-grown person in the eye.
- Snakes have flexible jaws that allow them to swallow prey larger than their heads by unhinging their lower jaw.
- Horned desert vipers have heat-sensing pits on their heads that allow pit vipers like rattlesnakes to accurately strike at warm-blooded prey in complete darkness.

- The Mozambique spitting cobra can spit venom over 8 feet away directly into the eyes of threats to blind them.
- Snakes have a slow metabolism that allows some species, like pythons, to survive on only 12 meals per year.
- Anacondas are semi-aquatic boa constrictors found in the rivers and swamps of the Amazon that can reach over 30 feet long.
- The inland taipan of Australia has the most toxic venom of any snake but is quite shy and rarely strikes humans.
- The twig snake's thin, cylindrical body and beige coloring allow it to perfectly camouflage itself as a dead stick in the forest.
- Snakes flick their forked tongue to collect scent particles and pass them to an organ in the roof of their mouth for analysis.
- Spitting cobras can spray venom from forward-facing holes in their fangs directly into the eyes of threats.
- The boomslang snake gets its name from the Afrikaans word for "tree snake," since it lives in trees and bushes across sub-Saharan Africa.
- Ball pythons curl into a tight ball when frightened, hiding their heads inside their coils for protection.
- Snakes use their flickering forked tongues to pick up scent particles from the air and ground to detect predators or prey.
- The garter snake is one of the most cold-tolerant snakes, found as far north as Alaska and Canada.
- Cobras can extend the skin behind their neck into a signature hood shape when threatened or agitated.
- Rattlesnakes rapidly shake their tails, producing an iconic buzzing rattle to warn off intruders.
- Bush vipers have long fangs that fold back against the roof of their mouth and can inject venom deep into prey.

- The black mamba is extremely fast and agile, capable of reaching speeds over 12 miles per hour.
- Sea snakes have paddle-shaped tails that enable them to swim effectively and hunt fish underwater.
- The king cobra is the world's longest venomous snake, capable of reaching 18 feet in length.
- Cobras can flare out the skin behind their heads into a signature hood when threatened.
- Viper snakes have long, hinged fangs that lie flat and then erect when the snake strikes to inject venom deep into prey.
- Pit vipers like copperheads and rattlesnakes have heat-sensing pits on their faces to detect warm-blooded prey.
- Spitting cobras can spit or spray venom from their fangs directly into the eyes of threats up to 8 feet away.
- Ball pythons will curl up into a tight ball, hiding their heads inside their coils, when frightened.
- Anacondas are semi-aquatic boa constrictors found in the Amazon that can grow over 30 feet long.
- The twig snake's thin body and beige color allow it to disguise itself perfectly as a dead stick in the jungle.
- The inland taipan of Australia has the most toxic venom of any snake, but is quite shy and rarely strikes humans.
- Snakes have flexible jaws that allow them to swallow prey larger than their heads by unhinging their lower jaw.
- Horned desert vipers have supraorbital horns above their eyes that give them a menacing appearance.
- The Mozambique spitting cobra can spit venom over 8 feet away directly into the eyes of threats to blind them.
- Snakes have slow metabolisms that allow some species, like pythons, to survive on just 12 meals per year.
- The common garter snake is one of the most cold-tolerant, found as far north as Alaska and Canada.

- Coral snakes have highly potent neurotoxic venom that paralyzes nerve cells, shutting down breathing and causing death.
- Heat-sensing pits on their heads allow pit vipers like rattlesnakes to accurately strike warm-blooded prey in darkness.
- The bushmaster snake has the longest venom fangs, measuring up to 2 inches long.
- The king cobra is capable of raising one-third of its body off the ground and looking a full-grown person in the eye.
- The black mamba is extremely fast and agile, capable of reaching speeds over 12 miles per hour.
- The Mozambique spitting cobra can spit venom from its fangs over 8 feet away directly into the eyes of threats to blind them.
- Horned desert vipers have distinctive horns above their eyes that give them a menacing appearance.
- Bushmasters have the longest venom fangs of any snake, measuring up to 2 inches in length.
- The inland taipan of Australia has the most toxic venom of any snake but is quite shy and rarely strikes humans.
- The common garter snake is highly cold-tolerant and is found as far north as Alaska and Canada during summer.
- Coral snakes possess a powerful neurotoxic venom that paralyzes nerve cells, shutting down breathing and causing suffocation.
- Horned desert vipers have distinctive supraorbital horns above their eyes, giving them a menacing look.
- Spitting cobras can spray venom from forward-facing holes in their hollow fangs as a defense.

Chapter 5: Jumping Frogs

- The starred-nose frog has an unusual star-shaped appendage protruding from its nose.
- The common frog has powerful hind legs that allow it to leap over 20 times its body length.
- Poison dart frogs get their name from indigenous tribes who would coat arrow tips with the toxins secreted from the frogs' skin.
- The Goliath frog is the largest frog species with some growing over 1 foot long and weighing up to 7 pounds.
- Red-eyed tree frogs have toe pads specially adapted to grip branches and leaves in the humid rainforests they inhabit.

- The Mexican burrowing toad spends the majority of its life underground and emerges only during the rainy season to breed.
- The paradoxical frog got its name because tadpoles are larger than the adult frogs they mature into.
- The pixie frog advertises its toxicity with bright colors to warn potential predators.
- Some frog species like the gray tree frog can survive freezing temperatures by producing a special antifreeze glycoprotein.
- Wallace's flying frog of Southeast Asia can glide up to 50 feet between trees using specially adapted webbed feet.
- The African bullfrog can eat prey up to 80 percent of its own size including mice, small snakes, and other frogs.
- The desert rain frog of Namibia burrows underground and only emerges for about a week during mating season after heavy rainfall.
- The Golden dart frog has enough toxin secreted from its skin to kill 10 grown men, making it one of the most poisonous animals alive.
- The Great Plains narrowmouth toad spends the hot and dry months of summer burrowing deep underground, up to 11 feet down.
- The glass frog has transparent abdominal skin through which its internal organs and musculature can be seen.
- The small, stout-legged toad has short, stout limbs, making it a poor jumper. Instead, it walks across forest floors in search of insects.
- The screaming frog genus got its name from the shrill, high-pitched calls the frogs emit, especially when fighting over mates.

- The Surinam toad gives birth through the skin of its back, with young emerging fully formed as tiny toads rather than tadpoles.
- Flying tree frogs can glide as far as 50 feet between trees thanks to their webbed hands and feet stretching out skin flaps.
- The Darwin frog male swallows the eggs after the female lays them, incubates them in its vocal sac, and later coughs up fully formed frogs.
- The waxy monkey tree frog secretes a waxy substance over its skin to keep from drying out in the hot tropical climates where it lives.
- The concave-eared torrent frog has specially adapted ears to help it hear over the roar of the rocky streams it lives near.
- The pouched frog gets its name from the unique bilaterally located skin pouches on the lower back of the male for carrying the fertilized eggs.
- The African bullfrog can eat prey up to 80 percent of its own size, including mice, small snakes, and other frogs.
- The paradoxical frog's tadpoles are significantly larger than the adult frogs they eventually morph into.
- Wallace's flying frog can glide up to 50 feet between trees using specially adapted webbed hands and feet.
- The Great Plains narrowmouth toad stays burrowed up to 11 feet underground through hot, dry summer months.
- The golden poison frog secretes enough toxin through its skin to kill up to 10 adult humans.
- The glass frog has translucent abdominal skin, so its internal organs and digestive system can be seen through the underside.

- The Hula painted frog was thought to be extinct for over 50 years until it was rediscovered in 2011 in the Hula Valley of Israel.
- The crimson-snouted tree frog spends most of its time in trees and has specialized toe pads for climbing and gripping branches.
- The green and black poison dart frog gets its toxicity from consuming a diet of alkaloid-laden insects like ants and mites.
- The marsupial frog carries its eggs in a pouch on its back until they hatch, whereas most frogs lay eggs directly in water.
- The hairy frog breaks its own bones and claws to create sharp points that puncture through the frog's skin for self-defense.
- The desert rain frog can wait underground for years during drought conditions until the next period of rainfall.
- The pancake tortoise earned its name from its exceptionally flat shell and body, which are adapted for slipping into rock crevices.
- The Surinam toad gives birth through the skin of its back, with young emerging fully formed as tiny toads.
- The paradoxical frog's tadpoles are larger than the tiny adult frogs they eventually morph into.
- The blue-tongued leaf frog has a bright turquoise-blue tongue that it displays to scare away predators.
- The gastric-brooding frog swallows its eggs, stops secreting stomach acid, and incubates the eggs in its stomach until they hatch.
- The African bullfrog can eat prey up to 80 percent of its size, including mice, smaller frogs, lizards, and small snakes.

- The golden poison frog secretes enough toxin through its skin to kill up to 10 grown men, making it extremely poisonous.
- The Great Plains narrowmouth toad spends hot, dry months burrowing underground, up to 11 feet down.
- The desert rain frog emerges for just about a week after rare rainstorms, otherwise spending years underground.
- The screaming frog gets its name from the shrill, high-pitched mating call the male frogs emit when competing for mates.
- The hairy frog breaks its own toe bones and claws to create sharp points that puncture through the skin for self-defense.
- The concave-eared torrent frog has specially adapted ears to help it hear over the sound of rushing streams it lives near.
- The marsupial frog carries its eggs in a pouch on its back until they hatch, whereas most frogs lay eggs in water.
- The paradoxical frog tadpoles are significantly larger than the tiny adult frogs they eventually morph into.
- The pouched frog male has bilaterally located skin pouches on its lower back for carrying fertilized eggs.
- The spotted grass frog is well camouflaged in grasslands, with olive green skin flecked with brown spots.
- The desert rain frog can remain underground through years of drought before emerging after rare rainfall.
- The green and black poison dart frog gets its toxins from eating alkaloid-rich ants, mites, and beetles.
- The crimson-snouted tree frog has specialized toe pads for climbing and gripping branches.
- The gastric brooding frog incubated its eggs in its stomach by stopping stomach acid secretion.

- The Darwin's frog male incubates the eggs in its vocal sac after the female lays them, later coughing up fully formed frogs.
- The glass frog has translucent abdominal skin, so its organs and digestive system are visible through its underside.
- The waxy monkey tree frog secretes wax over its skin to prevent it from drying out in the hot tropical climates where it lives.
- The pouched frog male has bilaterally located skin pouches on its lower back for carrying fertilized eggs.
- The hairy frog breaks its own bones and claws to create sharp points that puncture through the skin for defense.
- The golden poison frog secretes enough toxin through its skin to kill up to 10 grown men.
- The Great Plains narrowmouth toad stays burrowed up to 11 feet underground through hot, dry summers.
- The African bullfrog can eat prey up to 80 percent of its size including mice, smaller frogs, lizards, and small snakes.
- The screaming frog gets its name from the shrill, high-pitched mating call the male frogs emit when competing for mates.
- The marsupial frog carries its eggs in a pouch on its back until they hatch, unlike most frogs.
- The hairy frog punctures its own skin with sharp claws for self-defense against predators.
- The waxy monkey tree frog secretes wax over its skin to prevent drying out in hot, tropical climates.
- The pouched frog male has skin pouches on its lower back for carrying fertilized eggs.
- The hairy frog breaks its own bones and claws to create sharp points that puncture through its skin for defense.

- The blue-tongued leaf frog displays its bright blue tongue to scare away predators when threatened.
- The gastric-brooding frog incubated its eggs in its stomach by temporarily stopping stomach acid secretion.
- The African bullfrog can eat prey up to 80 percent of its size, including mice, smaller frogs, lizards, and small snakes.

Chapter 6: Swimming Fish

- The great white shark is the largest predatory fish on Earth, growing over 20 feet long and weighing up to 5,000 pounds.
- Electric eels can generate powerful electric shocks up to 860 volts to stun prey and defend themselves.
- Seahorses have a distinctive upright posture with a curled prehensile tail that allows them to anchor themselves to sea grasses and corals.
- Pufferfish inflate themselves like balloons by gulping water when threatened to appear larger to predators.
- The Mekong giant catfish is one of the world's largest freshwater fish, weighing over 600 pounds.

- Male seahorses have a pouch on their belly that they use to incubate fertilized eggs from the female.
- Hatchetfish get their name from their distinctively shaped bodies that are flat on the bottom and arched on top like a hatchet blade.
- Flying fish can glide through the air for hundreds of feet above the water's surface by beating their large pectoral fins.
- Archerfish use jets of water to knock insects and spiders into the water from branches hanging over the surface.
- The coelacanth was thought to be extinct for 65 million years until a living specimen was caught off the coast of South Africa in 1938.
- The ocean sunfish is the heaviest known bony fish in the world, with some reaching over 5,000 pounds.
- Anglerfish have a glowing lure dangling over their mouths to attract prey in the darkness of the deep ocean depths.
- Salmon migrate from the ocean upstream to spawn in the exact freshwater rivers and streams where they hatched years before.
- The freshwater stingray has a barbed, venomous stinger, making it potentially hazardous to waders despite its small size.
- Lungfish can breathe air through a special lung-like organ, allowing them to survive for years out of water if their habitat dries up.
- The stonefish is well camouflaged in coral reefs and has venomous spines used to sting potential predators.
- The leafy seadragon sways back and forth, mimicking floating seaweed, to help conceal itself near seagrasses and kelp beds.

- The moray eel has two sets of jaws: a main jaw for capturing prey and a second jaw that shoots forward when the main one opens.
- Mudskippers are amphibious fish that can spend days out of water, skipping and slithering around on their modified pectoral fins.
- Lanternfish have light-producing organs called photophores that provide camouflage by matching the light down in the deep ocean.
- The great white shark is the largest predatory fish on Earth, growing over 20 feet long and weighing up to 5,000 pounds.
- Swordfish have a sword-like protrusion on their faces that allows them to slash and stun prey before eating them.
- Electric eels can generate powerful electric shocks of up to 860 volts to stun prey and defend themselves.
- Archerfish knock insects and spiders into the water from overhanging branches by shooting water jets.
- Seahorses have a curled, prehensile tail that allows them to anchor themselves to seagrasses and corals.
- Clownfish form a symbiotic relationship with sea anemones, protected by the anemones' stinging tentacles as they clean them.
- The coelacanth was thought to have been extinct for 65 million years until a living one was caught off Africa's coast in 1938.
- Anglerfish have a glowing lure dangling over their mouths to attract prey in the darkness of the deep sea.
- The leafy seadragon sways like seaweed to camouflage itself near seagrasses and kelp beds.
- Salmon migrate upstream to spawn in the exact freshwater rivers and streams where they hatch.

- The ocean sunfish is the heaviest known bony fish, with some reaching over 5,000 pounds.
- Lungfish can breathe air through a specialized lung organ, allowing them to survive for years out of water if their habitat dries up.
- Hatchetfish get their name from their distinctively shaped bodies, which are flat on the bottom and arched on top.
- The freshwater stingray has a barbed, venomous stinger, making it hazardous to waders despite its small size.
- Male seahorses have a pouch on their belly that they use to incubate fertilized eggs from females.
- Mudskippers are amphibious fish that can skip and slither around on land for days using their modified fins.
- Lanternfish have light-producing photophores that provide camouflage, matching the light down in the deep sea.
- The great white shark is the largest predatory fish on Earth, growing over 20 feet long and weighing up to 5,000 pounds.
- Archerfish knock insects and spiders into the water from overhanging branches by shooting water jets.
- Seahorses have a curled, prehensile tail that allows them to anchor themselves to seagrasses and corals.
- Pufferfish inflate themselves by gulping water when threatened, to appear larger to predators.
- Anglerfish have a glowing lure dangling above their mouths to attract prey in the pitch black depths.
- Salmon migrate upstream to spawn in the exact freshwater rivers and streams where they hatched.
- The leafy seadragon sways like seaweed to camouflage itself near seagrasses and kelp beds.
- The ocean sunfish is the heaviest known bony fish in the world, with some reaching over 5,000 pounds.

- Male seahorses have a pouch on their belly that they use to incubate fertilized eggs from females.
- Clownfish form a symbiotic relationship with sea anemones, protected by the anemones' stinging tentacles.
- Salmon migrate upstream to spawn in the exact rivers and streams where they hatched.
- The leafy seadragon sways like seaweed to camouflage itself near seagrasses and kelp beds.

Chapter 7: Extinct Beasts

- Tyrannosaurus rex was one of the largest and most fearsome carnivores ever to live, weighing over 6 tons and growing 40 feet long.
- Wooly mammoths had thick, shaggy coats and long curved tusks used to clear snow from vegetation during the last ice age.
- Saber-toothed tigers had up to 8-inch canine teeth used for slashing and piercing the flesh of their prey.
- Giant ground sloths grew to 20 feet long, used their massive claws for digging, and had thick armor-like skin.
- Triceratops had three sharp horns on its head, along with a bony frill that may have been used for defense and display.
- Pterodactyls were flying reptiles with enormous wingspans, with the largest being over 30 feet across.

- The Megalodon shark was one of the most fearsome predators of all time, growing over 60 feet long with teeth the size of a human hand.
- Brachiosaurus was one of the tallest and heaviest dinosaurs, with some adults weighing over 80 tons.
- Ankylosaurus was covered in hard, bony plates and had a club-like tail used as a powerful defensive weapon.
- Velociraptors were feathered carnivores that hunted in packs and had a deadly hooked claw on each foot for grappling prey.
- Stegosaurus had distinctive double rows of diamond-shaped bony plates along its back and wielded a spiked tail.
- Quetzalcoatlus was one of the largest flying animals ever, with a wingspan over 30 feet wide.
- Parasaurolophus had an elongated, tube-like crest connected to its nostrils, which may have produced resonant sounds.
- The enormous shell of Archelon was over 4 meters long, making it the largest sea turtle that ever existed.
- Euoplocephalus could swing its heavily armored tail club defensively at predators like the Tyrannosaurus.
- Giganotosaurus was heavier and longer than T. rex, with more powerful jaws but smaller arms.
- Entelodonts, also called "hell pigs," were ancient omnivorous mammals the size of a rhinoceros.
- Dimetrodon is often mistaken for a dinosaur but was actually a pelycosaur, an early synapsid reptile predating dinosaurs.
- Deinonychus were fast, deadly pack hunters, with a retractable 12-inch claw on each foot used for disemboweling prey.

- Mosasaurs were gigantic marine reptiles rivaling modern whales, with paddle-like limbs and powerful jaws.
- Tyrannosaurus rex was one of the largest and most fearsome carnivores ever, weighing over 6 tons and growing 40 feet long.
- Wooly mammoths had thick, shaggy coats and long, curved tusks used to clear snow from vegetation during the last ice age.
- Saber-toothed tigers had up to 8-inch canine teeth used for slashing and piercing the flesh of prey.
- Giant ground sloths grew to 20 feet long, used massive claws for digging, and had thick armor-like skin.
- Triceratops had three sharp horns on its head and a bony frill that may have been used for defense and display.
- Pterodactyls were flying reptiles with enormous wingspans, the largest being over 30 feet across.
- The Megalodon shark grew over 60 feet long with teeth the size of a human hand, making it one of the most fearsome predators ever.
- Brachiosaurus was one of the tallest and heaviest dinosaurs, with some adults weighing over 80 tons.
- Velociraptors were feathered carnivores that hunted in packs and had a deadly hooked claw on each foot.
- Stegosaurus had distinctive double rows of diamond-shaped bony plates along its back and wielded a spiked tail.
- Quetzalcoatlus was one of the largest flying animals ever, with a wingspan over 30 feet wide.
- Parasaurolophus had a long, tube-like crest connected to its nostrils, which may have produced resonant sounds.
- The enormous shell of Archelon was over 4 meters long, making it the largest sea turtle to have existed.

- Euoplocephalus could swing its heavily armored tail club defensively at predators like Tyrannosaurus.
- Giganotosaurus was heavier and longer than T. rex, with more powerful jaws but smaller arms.
- Entelodonts, also called "hell pigs," were ancient omnivorous mammals the size of rhinos.
- Dimetrodon is often mistaken for a dinosaur but was actually an early synapsid reptile predating dinosaurs.
- Deinonychus were fast, deadly pack hunters with 12-inch claws on each foot used for disemboweling prey.
- Mosasaurs were giant marine reptiles rivaling modern whales, with paddle-like limbs and jaws.
- Tyrannosaurus rex was one of the largest and most fearsome carnivores ever, weighing over 6 tons and growing 40 feet long.
- Woolly mammoths had thick, shaggy coats and long curved tusks used to clear snow from vegetation during the last ice age.
- Saber-toothed tigers had up to 8-inch canine teeth used for slashing and piercing the flesh of prey.
- Giant ground sloths grew to 20 feet long, used massive claws for digging, and had thick armor-like skin.
- Triceratops had three sharp horns on its head and a bony frill that may have been used for defense and display.
- Pterodactyls were flying reptiles with enormous wingspans, the largest over 30 feet across.
- The megalodon shark grew over 60 feet long with teeth the size of a human hand - one of the most fearsome predators ever.
- Brachiosaurus was one of the tallest and heaviest dinosaurs, with some adults weighing over 80 tons.
- Velociraptors were feathered carnivores that hunted in packs and had a deadly hooked claw on each foot.

- Stegosaurus had distinctive double rows of diamond-shaped bony plates along its back and wielded a spiked tail.
- Parasaurolophus had a long, tube-like crest connected to its nostrils which may have produced resonant sounds.
- The enormous shell of Archelon was over 4 meters long, making it the largest sea turtle to have existed.
- Euoplocephalus could swing its heavily armored tail club defensively at predators like Tyrannosaurus.
- Giganotosaurus was heavier and longer than T. rex, with more powerful jaws but smaller arms.
- Entelodonts, also called "hell pigs," were ancient omnivorous mammals the size of rhinos.
- Dimetrodon is often mistaken for a dinosaur but was actually an early synapsid reptile predating dinosaurs.
- Deinonychus were fast, deadly pack hunters with 12-inch claws on each foot used for disemboweling prey.
- Mosasaurs were giant marine reptiles rivaling modern whales, with paddle-like limbs and jaws.
- Tyrannosaurus rex was one of the largest and most fearsome carnivores ever, weighing over 6 tons and growing 40 feet long.
- Wooly mammoths had thick, shaggy coats and long, curved tusks used to clear snow from vegetation during the last ice age.
- Saber-toothed tigers had up to 8-inch canine teeth used for slashing and piercing the flesh of prey.
- Giant ground sloths grew to 20 feet long, used massive claws for digging, and had thick armor-like skin.
- Brachiosaurus was one of the tallest and heaviest dinosaurs, with some adults weighing over 80 tons.
- Deinonychus were fast, deadly pack hunters with 12-inch claws on each foot used for disemboweling prey.

- The Helicoprion, an extinct shark, had a unique "tooth-whorl" structure that spiraled out from its lower jaw.
- The Glyptodon, a prehistoric relative of armadillos, had a massive, domed shell that could reach up to 6 feet in diameter.
- Thylacine, also known as the Tasmanian Tiger, was the largest carnivorous marsupial and is now extinct.
- The Dodo bird's closest living relative is the Nicobar pigeon.
- Quagga, a half-striped zebra, was declared extinct in the late 19th century.
- The Irish Elk had the largest antlers of any known deer species, with a span of up to 12 feet.
- The Archaeopteryx is considered the first bird, known for its mix of bird and dinosaur-like features.
- The Moa, a giant flightless bird from New Zealand, could stand up to 12 feet tall.
- The Steller's Sea Cow was a massive marine mammal that measured up to 30 feet and was hunted to extinction.
- The Elasmotherium, or Siberian Unicorn, was a horned prehistoric rhinoceros.
- The Great Auk was a large, flightless seabird that went extinct in the 19th century.
- Haast's Eagle from New Zealand was the largest eagle known to have existed.
- The Chinese Paddlefish, once found in the Yangtze River, is one of the most recently extinct animals.
- The Thylacoleo, or Marsupial Lion, was a powerful predator from ancient Australia.
- The Moeritherium, a prehistoric elephant ancestor, was adapted for both land and water.

- The Falkland Islands Wolf was the only native land mammal in the Falkland Islands and became extinct in the 19th century.
- The Short-Faced Bear was one of the largest terrestrial mammalian carnivores in North America.
- The Sea Mink, native to North America, was the only mink species adapted to a marine lifestyle.
- The Jamaican Iguana was once considered extinct but was rediscovered in 1990.
- Humans hunted the Steller's Sea Cow, which has been extinct since the 18th century, for its blubber.
- The Gastornis, often called the "Terror Bird," was a flightless bird that lived around 56 to 33 million years ago.
- The Barbary Lion was a subspecies of lion that went extinct in the wild in the 20th century.
- The Macrauchenia was a bizarre mammal resembling a mix of a camel and a tapir.
- The Tasmanian Tiger had a pouch similar to that of marsupials, despite being a carnivorous predator.
- The Woolly Rhinoceros, a cold-adapted species, was covered in a thick coat of fur.
- The Megatherium, a giant ground sloth, could reach up to 20 feet in length.
- The Palaeopropithecus, an extinct lemur from Madagascar, had a sloth-like appearance.
- The Doedicurus, a large glyptodont, had a spiked tail club for self-defense.
- The Gorgonopsids were saber-toothed reptiles that lived during the Permian period.
- Opabinia was a strange marine arthropod with five eyes and a unique proboscis.
- The Titanoboa was the largest snake ever known to exist, with an estimated length of 40–50 feet.

- The Cuvieronius, a relative of modern-day elephants, inhabited South America during the Pleistocene epoch.
- Carcharocles Chubutensis, also known as "Megalodon's cousin," was a prehistoric shark.
- The Dromornis was a giant flightless bird from Australia, nicknamed the "Thunder Bird."
- The Pyrenean Ibex was the first animal to be briefly brought back from extinction through cloning before its death in 2000.
- The Dusicyon, or Falkland Islands Wolf, was the only native land mammal in the Falkland Islands.
- The Phorusrhacids, also known as "Terror Birds," were large, flightless birds that were formidable predators.
- Leiolopisma, an extinct skink, had elongated limbs and a snake-like body.
- The Deinosuchus, a giant prehistoric alligator, preyed on dinosaurs.
- The Archaeoindris, an extinct lemur, was the largest known primate that ever lived.
- The Xerces Blue, a butterfly species, became the first American butterfly to go extinct due to human activity.
- The Woolly Mammoth was one of the last surviving species of the Ice Age megafauna.
- The Indricotherium, also known as Paraceratherium, was the largest land mammal that ever existed.
- Thylacosmilus was a marsupial saber-toothed predator from South America.
- The Ichthyornis was an ancient bird with a toothed beak.
- Andrewsarchus was a large carnivorous mammal that lived during the Eocene epoch.
- The Protarchaeopteryx was a feathered dinosaur from China, known as the "dawn feather."

- The Tasmanian Tiger's scientific name is Thylacinus cynocephalus, meaning "pouched dog with a wolf's head."
- The Haast's Eagle preyed on the flightless Moa birds in New Zealand and had a wingspan of over 10 feet.

.

Check out Dr. Leo Lexicon's most popular release and read an excerpt:
AI for Smart Kids Ages 6-9

WHAT YOU WILL LEARN

✓ Discover: What is AI and how is it used in everyday life
✓ Explore: From Narrow AI to Super AI, meet AI's real superpowers
✓ Dive into AI history: Meet the Key Inventors, from ancient times to today
✓ Understand: Data, machine learning, and programming, the building blocks of AI
✓ Imagine the future with AI: Education, jobs, creativity, ethics, and beyond. Get involved!

Scan the QR Code to order the book now!

DR. LEO LEXICON
AI FOR SMART KIDS
AGES 6-9
DISCOVER HOW
ARTIFICIAL INTELLIGENCE
IS CHANGING THE WORLD

EXCERPT

Chapter 2: The Types of AI

Defining AI

Let us start the chapter by agreeing on how to define AI. We already talked about some examples that show you how AI actually works. In general, when computers are programmed to be extremely intelligent and perform tasks that typically require human intelligence, such as learning, problem-solving, and decision-making, this is known as artificial intelligence, or AI. This is the working definition of AI we will use for the rest of the book.

Typically, we can think of three types of AI: narrow AI, general AI, and super AI. Let us take a look at what we mean by these:

Narrow AI

Narrow AI is comparable to a computer that does well at only one specific task. It is similar to being an expert in a particular task, like understanding Egyptian hieroglyphs, or knowing all about planes, for example. Now consider a computer that is particularly good at playing the game of chess. It is a master chess player who is familiar with all the moves and tactics, and has learned how to play by analyzing thousands, if not millions, of games. However, because it is so focused on chess, if you asked it to do something else, like ride a bicycle or paint a picture, it wouldn't know how to do those things.

Another well-known example is a computer that can scan images and tell you whether a cat is present. This has actually been tried out at top technology companies as a test to see if the AI actually works. This computer can quickly respond, "Yes, there's a cat!" or "No, there isn't!" when you show it a picture because it has been trained to recognize what a cat looks like. However, due to its focus on finding cats, if you asked it to do something else, like tell you if an elephant was present in the image or count the number of trees in another image, it would be unable to do so.

General AI

The next type of AI we will look at is General AI. Now, General AI is similar to having a computer that is extremely intelligent, just like a very smart person. It has a wide range of abilities (as opposed to narrow ones), just like humans do. It can pick up new information, comprehend what it sees, and even perform tasks that we haven't explicitly taught it how to do. So, as you can see, it is quite different from narrow AI.

Think of a friend you have who is very intelligent and versatile. They are capable of telling jokes, playing sports, doing math, and painting stunning works of art. Everything they put their mind to, it seems like they pick up that skill very fast. That is how general AI operates. It can learn from humans and comprehend the knowledge we possess, enabling it to assist us with a variety of tasks.

Say you teach the general AI how to play the game of chess. Like the narrow AI whom we met earlier and who was an expert at playing chess, the general AI will pick up the game and get really good at it. The interesting part is that the general AI can also pick up other games like checkers or tic-tac-toe without having been explicitly taught those games. It can learn how to play new games by applying the knowledge it already possesses and using its powers of observation and analysis.

General AI is also capable of human-like comprehension. It can be taught to recognize various objects, animals, and even the definitions of words and sentences. It can therefore perform many tasks just like us and is comparable to a really smart computer friend. Even though we haven't taught it yet, it is capable of learning, comprehending, and performing new tasks. It's like having a super-smart assistant who can help us with a variety of tasks. You can now begin to see how general AI is a big leap from narrow AI. It can suddenly help us explore so many new areas and become a trusted assistant or co-pilot.

Super AI

Now, let's talk about the big kahuna: Super AI! Imagine being able to ask a computer any question and having the answer provided right away. Or if you could give it a particularly challenging mathematical equation to solve, it would quickly solve it. All of that and a whole lot more would be possible with super AI! No problem, however complex, is beyond its capacity to solve. It is like having a genius on speed dial.

Scientists are still working on developing super AI, but it might take some time given how difficult it is. They want to make sure it is secure and has practical applications. They want to be extremely cautious and ensure that there won't be any issues that cause things to go wrong. We will get to the reasons why we need to be very careful while developing a capability like Super AI in a later chapter.

University research labs, companies, and the government are all spending millions of dollars every year on this research. And who knows? Perhaps we will soon have computers that are much smarter than anyone could have ever imagined. It is a fascinating concept to consider!

Now that we know what AI is, and what the different types of AI can do, it is important to understand that it took many years of research and the work of many brilliant minds to get here. In the next chapter, we will look at the brief history of AI.

Don't miss our upcoming title:
AI for Smart Pre-Teens Ages 10-12

Check Dr. Leo Lexicon's Author Page on Amazon.com for updates and new releases!

More titles for Smart Kids!

- Each book has over 40+ carefully curated HQ images
- Pefect companion for a road trip or vacation
- Try one today, you won't be disappointed
- Check out our other titles, we have all ages covered
- From the team at Lexicon Labs, bringing joy one page at a time!
- Follow Dr. Leo Lexicon on Twitter

@LeoLexicon

Printed in Great Britain
by Amazon